Rossington Remembered

Glimpses into the Past
(Book 3)

Compiled by Frank Clarke

OLD VILLAGE SCENE.

ROSSINGTON

VILLAGE CHURCH AND GROUNDS.

To Annette, Elizabeth and Andrew.

ISBN: 0 9511307 2 2

Front cover: from a watercolour of Littleworth Lane
by Mr Peter Rouse.

Published by the Parochial Church Council of
St. Michael's Church, Rossington
on Sunday 18th September, 1994, in the presence
of the Bishop of Doncaster,
The Rt. Rev. Michael Gear.

Printed by G. W. Belton Ltd
Heaton Street Gainsborough
Lincs. DN21 2ED
Tel.0427 612291 Fax. 0427 810520

Preface

In "Rossington - More Glimpses into the Past", I suggested that there might be enough photographs for a third volume, and here it is. Pictures started coming in soon after the last book was published in 1990 and the flow has continued to provide me with the selection presented here. I make no apology that the majority are of people because people make history. As with the last book, there have again been one or two exciting finds: Sheepbridge Lane before most of the housing development took place; St. Michael's School prior to the 1963 alterations being made; Dr and Mrs Graftdyke; shows and pantomimes; pit officials in 1926; and a whole collection of Secondary Modern Boys' School photographs. I am sorry that a few views of the village which I know exist have not been included, but they were not offered!

Compiling the book has given me a lot of pleasure. I hope it gives many happy hours and brings back memories to everyone who reads it.

Again I have relied on the people who have lent their photographs to put names to faces; if they are incorrect or are spelled wrongly, I apologise. Where names have been omitted I am sure there will be many readers who will be able to add the missing information.

I still believe that Rossington is deserving of a full and detailed history; perhaps one day someone will write it! Meanwhile, enjoy book three and remember, please preserve your photographs for your family, and us, to enjoy.

Frank Clarke
September 1994.

Acknowledgements

I must begin by apologising to those people who lent photographs for "Rossington - More Glimpses into the Past" and whose names were omitted from the acknowledgements in that volume: Dr and Mrs Johnson of Bawtry, and Mr Bill Winfield.

On this occasion thanks are due to Mr Alan Barry, Mrs M. Billington, Mr A. Briggs, The Rt. Hon. J. D. Concannon, PC., Mr O. Cooke, Mrs Derbyshire, Mrs D. Dolman, Doncaster Library Service, Mrs I. Halford, Mr A. Harvey, Mrs Herme, Mrs Holt, Mrs Jenkinson, Mrs J. F. Kay, Mrs J. McGrane, Mrs F. McGuinness, Mrs M. Marrison, Mr R. Marsh, Mr E. Pearson, Mrs E. Phelps, Mr D. Quirk, Mr J. Righton, Mr P. Rouse, Mr B. Royle, the late Commander and Mrs N. Scarlett-Streatfeild, Miss P. Shiffner, Mrs M. Smith, Mrs J. Stacey, Mr N. Stanley, Mr J. Stones, Mrs M. Woodhouse, Mrs M. Woolrich, Mr C. Worsdale.

My thanks too to the Reverend Marc Seccombe and to the Parochial Church Council of St. Michael's for agreeing to publish a third book in the 150th anniversary year of the rebuilding of the Church by Mr James Brown in 1844. Also to our printer, G. W. Belton of Gainsborough. And last but not least, thank you to my wife, Annette, for her help and to Elizabeth and Andrew for their patience.

Frank Clarke

Foreword

This is the third book of Rossington "photographic memories" compiled and produced by Frank Clarke. Of course, it couldn't be done without the contributions of many people from Rossington - past and present,

Records of this kind are vitally important, as they collate together in an ordered fashion the individual and corporate memories of a community. Over the past few years, vast changes have taken place in the community that forms Rossington. So it is good to look back and remember its "roots". And, as always, such "roots" are really the people who have made, and continue to make the community.

It is good too that the Parochial Church Council publishes this book. Even now, despite all the changes and the fall away from "organised religion", people look to the Parish Church as a symbol of community and hope. Many still celebrate their significant family occasions by coming to the church (that has stood here for hundreds of years) - a sign of our being ultimately "rooted" in the family of God?

1994 is a special year for St Michael's, as it is 150 years since the church had a major re-building programme. In 1844, the owner of Rossington Hall (James Brown) took the responsibility of restoring the then dilapidated church; paying the huge cost out of his own pocket. So it is appropriate to publish this book to mark the celebration. Nowadays, there are no wealthy benefactors to put their hands in their pockets for the upkeep of the church. Now, it is up to members of the congregation, those who come to the Parish Church for their special occasions, and well-wishers in the community, to help support the church, financially.

This book too, will play its part. Profits from its sale will help maintain the fabric of our ancient church. So, thanks to Frank Clarke for his enthusiasm and hard work. Thanks to all who have contributed photos and notes, and thank you for purchasing it. If you have links with Rossington, I know you will enjoy it. And, who knows, there may yet be demand for a fourth!

Marc Seccombe
Rector (St Michael's, Rossington)
September 1994

Village Scenes

Rossington Bridge perhaps in the 1930's.

From the *Doncaster Gazette*, 12th May, 1939. The hotel was never built but the date gives a clue to when the old farm buildings were demolished for road widening.

The Brick Pond, bottom centre, and Jackson's estate on Yew Tree Crescent with *Yew Tree Farm, Ivy House Farm and Gattison Grange* still in evidence, date this view before 1975. Note the still extensive Rectory grounds and the first houses under construction on Stripe Road. Brooke Motors and the swimming baths can be seen on the right, and Tornedale School at the top.

Taken before the station (top left) was demolished but after the supermarket was built on Gattison Lane. *Gattison House* has yet to be built adjacent to Tornedale School.

St. Michael's Church and School House c1920.

St. Michael's School before the first extensions were built in 1963. This room is now the entrance hall.

Looking from where the main school entrance is today.

St. Michael's School and house viewed from The Carriageway prior to 1963.

A view across the old school playground.

Looking down Sheepbridge Lane towards Littleworth Lane with *Manor Farm* on the right. Sometime after 1956.

Ivy House Farm and *Fountain Cottages* perhaps in the 1930's.

Fountain Cottages with *Ivy House Farm* on the right and the pump on the left. c1960.

A modern view of *Fountain Cottages* after the extension to the Post Office was built.

Looking towards the pump with *Ivy House Farm* on the left and the front wall of the police station on the right.

Gattison Grange which stood on the old village side of the railway was purchased by Mr Henderson at the 1939 sale and was demolished in about 1975.

A stone pillar reputedly from Doncaster's St. Mary Magdalene's Church, stood in Mrs Bonser's garden on Stripe Road.

Cripps Avenue, perhaps in the 1950's.

St. Luke's Church c 1952.

Pit sinking machinery at the colliery, September, 1912. *(Doncaster Gazette)*

The *Hippodrome* cinema on Queen Mary's Road c1960.

Elmfield House on Grange Lane was built as the colliery manager's house but in later years was administered by the Comprehensive School and used by local groups prior to its demolition in 1992/3. A supermarket has since been built on the site.

Rossington Colliery sometime before 1981.

Nelson Road shops in the late 1950's.

The Comprehensive School was built to accommodate the old Secondary Modern Boys' and Girls' Schools which transferred here in 1968 from what is now Holmescarr School. Note the former estate kennel house on the right and the, as yet, undeveloped Bond Street.

A lovely photograph of *Grange Farm* occupied at one time by the Jeffersons. The photograph dates from about 1910. The flower urns outside the front door are still in the family but in Cornwall.

School Days

Rossington School football team 1921. Back row, l. to r. - S. McGann, T. Wren, T. Foster, D. Jarvis, ??, G. Parker. Front row, l. to r. - L. Lievesley, J. Simms, W. Boden, T. Walker, H. Greenwood.? Ward.

A Junior School class c1930. Included are, back row l. to r. - K. Langford, V. Caller, G. Robson, H. Gardner, N. Curry, E. Cantrill, B. Gardner, W. Bradshaw, 2nd from back, l. to r. - D. Melvin, B. West, H. Oakley, R. Reaney, J. Dove, E. Pearson. 3rd from back, l. to r. -?Dunlop, K. Simpson, C. Taylor, J. Grogan, F. Yates, O. Crummock, T. Andrews, ? Swift. 2nd from front, l. to r. - ? Rostron, F. Boyce, F. Antcliffe, ? Crooks, E. Bradley, E. Seymour. Front, l. to r. - H. Jackson, G. Hodgett, ? Lewis, C. Bell, D. Plaskett.

Junior School 1935. The back row includes, l. to r. - M. Pearson, M. Collins, J. Hughes, D. Burton, O. Charlton, J. McCaugh, A. Ainsworth, N. Hope, K. Jones. 2nd from back, l. to r. - M. Finch, J. Johnson, E. Creswick, C. Williams, V. Thompson, E. Watson. 3rd row, l. to r. - W. Taylor, R. Brown, E. Shepherd, K. Chivers, K. Needham, J. Yates, E. Meadows. 2nd from front, l. to r. - A. Evans, B. Bennett, D. Appleby, V. Clarke, A. Bains, K. Wildsmith, I. Langford, D. Basto, K. Guest. Front, l. to r. - L. Johnson, B. Smith, M. Bramhald, L. Spence, M. Wedd, E. Loftus.

A 1930's Boys' School class with Mr Fawcett (right).

Boys' School Class 2A, lower, in Jubilee Year 1935.

Boys School Class 1B in Coronation Year 1937. Fourth from the left on the third row is Clifford Morgan who emigrated to Australia in 1961.

Boys' School Class 3A in Coronation year. Lawrence Concannon at the left on the second row.

The nursery class held in the war years to allow mothers to work. Mrs Thomas (centre) was married to P.C. Thomas and lived in one of the houses behind the police station. Miss Hicky (left) was headmistress and Sheila Fynney, the nursery teacher.

ROSSINGTON is without a watchmaker, but the local residents do not worry about repairs. They have found the solution to their watch and clock problems, or rather Mr. J. C. Fawcett, the headmaster of Rossington Boys' Modern School, has found the solution for them, writes a "Chronicle" reporter who visited the school recently.

In the school science laboratory, in charge of Mr. Webster, the science master, senior boys in their last term are given the opportunity of using their hands and heads in doing all manner of household repairs—from sewing machines to electric irons, and kettles to gramophones, with a special department for the repair of watches and clocks. This is the department which at present, with a widespread shortage of watch repairers, is doing a roaring trade.

The repairs pour in. Mr. Webster told me that during the two years in which the science department has been open for this type of work, hundreds of watches and clocks, together with a multitude of other household effects, have been rapidly and efficiently dealt with, the result being that the School Red Cross Fund and the local Comforts Fund have benefited by over £70.

I looked in at the science room and found six of the senior pupils, mostly aged 13½ busily repairing, cleaning, and re-assembling watches and clocks of many shapes and sizes, ranging from pocket watches to grandmother clocks. On the "test-bench" were many others which had recently been repaired and were being tested for time-keeping—all ticking and tocking merrily away. And what a variety of sounds they made, from the rapid tick-tick-tick of the pocket watches to the slow ponderous tock-tock-tock of the big pendulum clock. All were registering the correct time.

No charge, of course, is made for the work done, it being left to the generosity of the "customers" as to the amount they drop into the Red Cross and Comforts Fund box.

Mr. Fawcett told me that the lads on this work—about a half dozen of them—are in their last term at school, and are excused most other school work to enable them to gain experience in household repair work. Other boys who are interested come along to the science room in their lunch hour to lend a hand.

"It's all grand experience for them," said Mr. Fawcett, and I agreed with him. We walked to another part of the laboratory, where boys were repairing a gramophone, while others were sharpening the teeth of saws with files.

"Nothing comes amiss to them," said Mr. Fawcett.

As I left the room the multitude of clocks seemed to me to echo his words —tick tick tick, nothing comes amiss, tock-tock-tock.   J.W.

From the *Doncaster Chronicle*. An article about a watch and clock repairing business operated at the Boys' School for the local comforts fund dates this to W.W. 2.

Boys' School about 1946, included are J. Hinds, D. Whitfield, D. Debenham, C. Finney, R. Cunningham, T. Often, ? Sargeant, D. Quirk, R. Lodge, Mr Kilburn, J. Nelmes, R.Higgins, R. Bales, D. Cooke, R. Monument, ? Catherall, ? Blake, Mr T. Scales, Mr F. Harris. A. Emberton, K. Taylor, B. Pendlebury, ? Allgold, J. Rylands, E. Elliott, K. Mann, A. Sarson, H. Blow, ? Pitchfork, ? Robinson, L. Beard, K. Smith.

A set of seven 1949/50 Boys' School groups pictured with Headmaster Mr Humphries, right. The first in the series includes Mr Waite, front right, Mr Cartlidge, second row left, and Mr Harris, front left.

Headmaster Mr Humphries with Mr Tom Williams, M.P. at a Boys' School prize day.

Some of the proud parents and pupils at the same prize day.

A Boys' School trip to the Festival of Britain in London, 1951.

On the Festival of Britain trip the boys were eager to be photographed with a London motorcycle bobby!

Mr Briggs with his class.

Another class photograph with Mr Briggs who first came to teach at the school in 1946.

A Junior School group in 1951 with M. Hinton, J. Ward, G. Merritt, B. Royle, P. Brady, and R. Lumb.

Sports day on the Welfare Grounds.

A school sports day cycle relay race, again at the Welfare

A Girls' School hockey team photographed on the Welfare Sports Ground with the Welfare building in the background.

Secondary Modern First Team Cup Winners c1952. Back row, l. to r. -Mel Job, Adrian Harvey, John Adametz, Ron Hinton, Alan Barry, Les Howbridge. Front row, l. to r. - Malc Clark, Cec Little, Ken Simpson, Tony Armstrong, Trevor Burns, The team beat Armthorpe 4 - 0 in the final.

Secondary Modern Intermediate Team, mid fifties. Back row, l. to r. - Mr R. Maye, Rob Punt, Ken Simpson, Trevor Burns, John Adametz, Rod Moody, Eddie Swift, Adrian Harvey, "Wink" Olive. Front, l. to r. - Ken Pointon, Jim Woods, Alan Barry, Ron Hinton, Cec Little, John Dunn.

Mr R. Maye with a 1955 -56 school soccer team including Geoff Palmer (Captain), Mike Armstone, Tibby Simpson, Graham Fiddler, Ian Lang, Ian Simms, Geof Palmer, Sam Pearson and Eric Bubb.

Secondary Modern Girls' School prefects c1955.
Back row, Valerie Scott, Rosemary Shepherd, Mrs Allan, Mrs Darlington, Rosemarie Wilkinson, Jean Andrew.
Front, Shirley Spacie, Carol Staley, Miss Halstead (Headmistress), Kathleen Rivers and Brenda Geddes.

Mr Maye with a Rossington's Doncaster School Rugby Champions, 1955. Glyn Jones, Phil Devlin, Joe Ward, Noel Dean, Harry Brown, Bill Summerill, Pete Duffy, Stanley Taylor, Bryan Royle, Robert Head, David Gardner, Syd Anderson, Derek Finch.

A Boys' School group c 1958/9 with teachers Mr Taylor and Mr J, Binns. Pupils include Alan Barry, Adrian Harvey, Malc Needham, Tony Tolliday, Dave Barron, Adrian Bailey, Raymond Spencer, Peter Skipp and Ron Hinton.

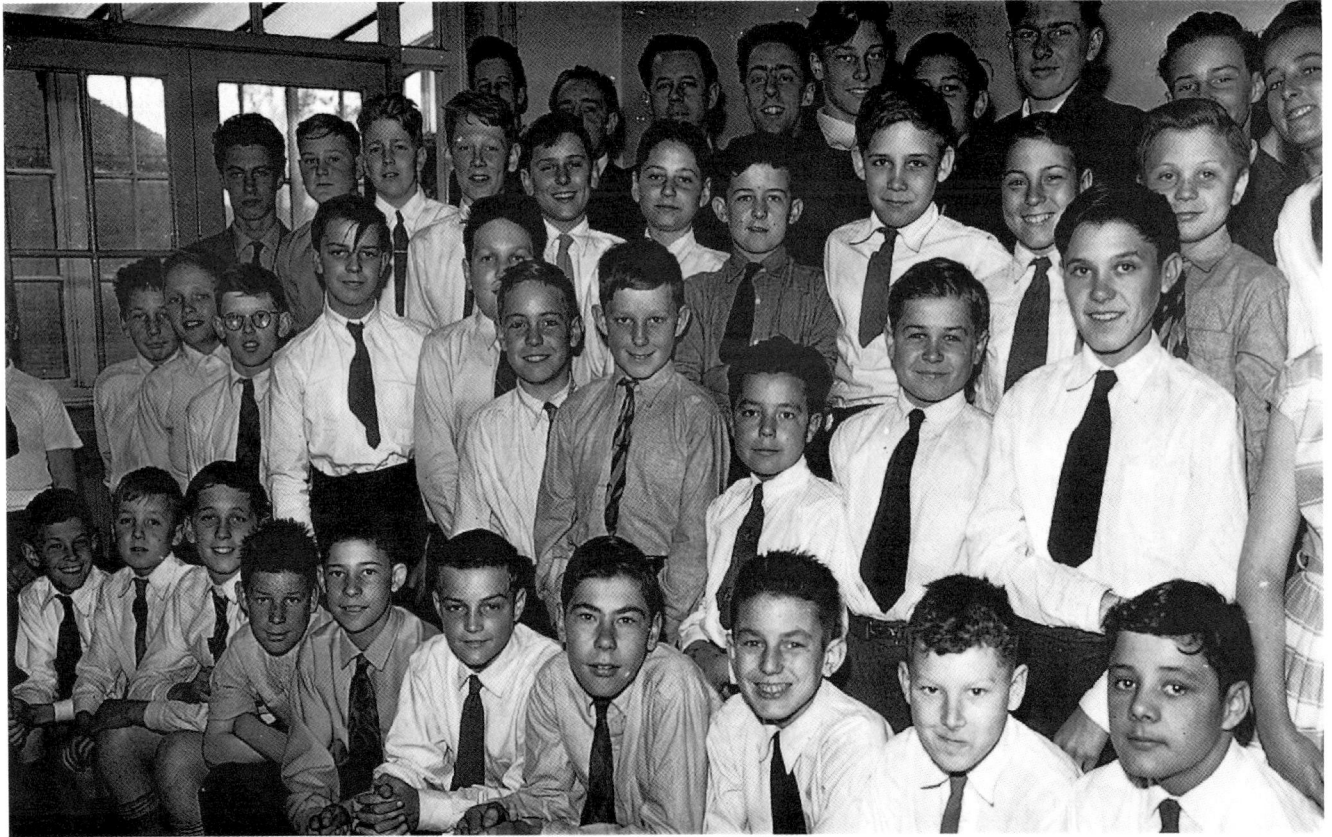

The Boys' School Senior Choir c 1959 with, staff, Mr R. Maye, Mr Binns and Mr Taylor. Among the pupils are 4th Formers Ron Hinton, Alan Barry, Adrian Harvey.

The Boys' School Staff. Mr Andrew Briggs, is on the front row, centre right and Mr Olive next to him. Mr Waite is on the front row, second from left.

Girls' School Hockey Team, second eleven 1959/60 with Mrs Allen (right) and Margaret Marrison (left).

The 1964 Girls' School Hockey Team. Christine Bailey, Judith Appleby, Kathryne Summerill, Mrs Dalton, Pat Harrison, Maria Bowziewsky, Brenda Taylor, Jenny Beaumont, Elizabeth Reynolds, Rita Dobson, Joan Davison, Anita Shaw.

Head Master Mr Peter Darvill on the front row, next to Mr Briggs, was Head of the new Comprehensive School.(now Rossington High School) Included in this photograph are the members of the school's first Sixth Form. The front row includes. - Mr 'Art' Taylor, Mr Waite, Mr 'Science' Taylor, Mrs Peggy Traber (Secretary), Mr Darvill, Mr Briggs, Mr Olive, Mr Fletcher. Middle row, centre, Mr Nunn and Mr Horn. Mr Darvill amalgamated the Girls' and Boys' Secondary Modern Schools to create the Comprehensive School

Headmaster Mr I. Howells, his wife, a teacher, and St. Michael's School pupils 1968. Mr Howells was Headmaster from 1966 until 1971.

Junior School canteen staff 1944 with, back row, Mrs Muggleston, Mrs Needham, Mrs Scarrow, Mrs Bell, Mrs Winter, Mrs Thompson, Mrs Weightman Front, Mrs Walker, Mrs Parker, Mrs Pritchard, Mrs Jenkinson (cook), Freda Smith and Alice Jones.

Boys' School canteen staff.

The Social Scene. May Day and Coronation Queens.

A 1940's May Queen.

Attendant Betty Vaux of *Manor Farm*, with an unidentified May Queen.

1948 May Queen with Eric Nichol, Bernard Nichol, Ron Nichol, Derek Jones, Len Finnegan, Freda McGuinness, Doreen Finnegan, Kathleen Wright, Dorothy Agar, Margaret Windle, Jill Webster, Jean Andrew, Jean Chessman, Annis Whiteley, Veronica McGuinness, Lynne Nichol, Wilf Andrew and Brian Jones.

Jean Mare, a 1950's May Queen with her retinue.

An as yet unidentified 1950's May Queen.

The 1952 May Queen Margaret Windle with Kathleen Wright, Doreen Finnegan, Lillian Finnegan, Audrey Wrightson, Len Finnegan and Derek Jones.

Grange Lane School 1953 Coronation Queen Marie Smith with her attendants.

Marie Smith again. Kay Hinton is also in this 1953 picture.

Catholic Church May Queen 1953, Merle Punt, with Marleine Picken, Wilf Andrew, David Summerill and Peter Tripp.

1953 May Queen Madge Dobson.

May Day 1954 or 1955.

A Dramatic Society production of about 1936 at the Welfare Hall. Included are R. Bramhald, G. Hall, ? Moore, M. Justice, J. Cunnah, Dr Kane, J. Lang, E. Clarke, Mrs Lang and E. Blount.

R. Jarvis, Gertrude Hall and J. Partington in an Operatic Society production. *(Merrie England ?)*

J. Lang, J. Partington and R. Jarvis in another unidentified Operatic Society show.

Miss Milbourne's youngest dancing troupe with Joyce Moss, May Bonser, J. Shepherd and Sheila Ward.

May Bonser and Joyce Moss dressed for a routine choreographed by Miss Millbourne and performed at the *Hippodrome* cinema during a talent week in the early part of W.W.2.

St. Luke's pantomime c1943 *Dick Whittington*. With Dorothy Overton, Charlie Burton, Margaret Bond, Jack Lievesley, Malcolm Roberts, Ronnie Lee, Jimmie Watson, Betty Askew and Joyce Moss.

The full cast of *Goodnight Vienna* with Harold Stevens on the back row (right) and including on the 2nd row, Mrs Stevens, Delia Mugglestone, Mrs Capper, Muriel Jackson, Tom Needham, Hilda Tripp Sn., Miss Holmes and Mrs Feltes.

On the front row can be seen Lydia O'Malley, Tom Bramhall, Gwenyth Edwards, Norman Stanley, Hilda Tripp Jn., Jean Williams, Gordon Crapper, Dorothy Overton, Reg Whalley, Nora Staley and Mr Crapper.

St. Luke's pantomime, 1946, *Ali Baba and the Forty Thieves.* Pictured here are Joan Lee, Joyce Appleby, Jean Calow, Mary and Norah Farmery, Joyce Moss, Jack Dyson, Horace Watson, Raymond Smith, Jack Lievesley and Jack Scales.

A local production of *Our Miss Gibbs* produced by Pansey Moore in 1947. Elsie Meadows, left, married Thomas Bramhald.

The full cast of *The Mikado* 1948.

Male members of the 1948 cast of *The Mikado*. Standing are Reg Whalley, Norman Holland and Joe Lowerson. Kneeling are Norman Stanley, Harley Kirsopp, Eddie Evans, Charlie Smith and Harold Evans.

A scene from *The Mikado* 1948 style with Jim Partington, Jean Williams, Albert Gent, Nora Staley, Hilda Tripp Jn., Tommy Bramhall, Eddie Evans and Mollie Whalley.

The full cast of *The Rebel Maid* performed in about 1949.

The Rebel Maid, l.to r. - Norah Staley, Mr Crapper, Eddie Evans, Charlie Wilson (kneeling), Norman Stanley, Gordon Crapper, Jean Williams. The man with the sergeant's stripes has not been identified.

Again *The Rebel Maid*, l. to r. - Gordon Crapper, Dorothy Overton, Jean Williams, Norman Stanley.

St. Luke's pantomime 1962, *Babes in York Wood* with Freda McAllister, Janet ?, Judy Appleby, Audrey ?, Pat ?, Susan ?, Barbara Freestone, Carol Tapson, Joan Davison and Lynne Spence.

Some of the cast from St. Luke's 1963 pantomime *Jack and the Beanstalk.*

Aladdin performed by the St. Luke's group in 1964. Pictured are Brian Tapson, Alan Moxon, Barry Gutteridge, Doug Needham, Pat Reid, Prue Staley, Janet Stacey, Cerris Blackshaw, Carol Moxon, Judy Appleby, Brian Royle, Robert Weekly and Barbara Freestone.

Gatherings and Groups

The Fitzwilliam Hounds met regularly in the village and here is a group outside the Rectory in 1909.

E.L.S. 1. MEET OF THE FITZWILLIAM HOUNDS AT ROSSINGTON, FEB 13TH 1909.

The same 1909 Meet with *Fountain Cottages* in the background.

MEET AT ROSSINGTON

Another view of the 1909 Meet looking down past the Rectory towards Littleworth Lane.

General William Bramwell Booth of the Salvation Army addressing a crowd outside the Co-op which opened in 1915.

The Stanley family on an outing to Cleethorpes about 1924.

Colliery officials during the 1926 strike. Back row, l. to r. - P. Pownall, A. Blount, F. Cusworth, S. Bradbury, T. Saxton, J. Leach, H. T. Webster, L. Lievesley, G. Wilkinson. Front, l. to r. - T. Clarkson, Stan Coe, H. Mettham, Sam Coe, J. Webster, H. Firth (Ambulanceman).

The local football team c 1929. Included are Henry Higgs, Dick Kelly, Tommy Stanley, "Mon" Matthews, Reg King and Walter Hartshorn.

Rossington Main Colliery Cricket XI in the early 1930's. Back row, l. to .r. - E. Clarkson, R. Kelly, A. Blount, W. Widdison, F. Jebson (Groundsman),D. Jarvis, F. Blount. Front, l. to r. - H. Lievesley, J. Harkin, L. Stanley, T. Stanley.

Ambulance Corp cadets and seniors photographed outside the old ambulance hut at the top of King George's Road in about 1932.

The Women's St. John's Ambulance Corp. Included are Mrs Tees, Mrs Needham, Mrs Whaley, Mrs Clark, Mrs Green and Mrs Jones.

A Christmas party at the Clinic in 1938.

RURAL DISTRICT COUNCIL ELECTION.
ROSSINGTON PARISH.

Polling Day, Saturday, April 1st, 1939.   8 a.m. to 8 p.m.

The Five Official Labour Candidates—**William Thomas Eade, Robert Edwin Hughes, Lewis Jones, Joshua Gabbittas McCague, Thomas Norman Stanley**— ask for your support and help to make Rossington 100 per cent. Labour seats on the Doncaster Rural District Council.

An election handbill for 1939.

The first W.W.2 'militia', July 1939. George Woodhouse, centre.

The Home Guard on parade in Queen Mary's Road passing the Market Place with the "Top Club" in the background. The photographer must have been standing in front of the *Hippodrome.*

Presentation of drums to the Air Training Corp, April 1945. Alderman Hughes is seated behind the drums.

May Day - the Labour Party Women's Section in about 1948 with Mrs Brain, Mrs Wareing, Mrs Teasdale, Mrs Nichol, Mrs McGuinness, Mrs Windle, Mrs Dobson, Mrs Wright, Mrs Jones, Mrs Finnegan and Peggy Webster (centre, front).

Members of the Labour Party Women's Section, again sometime in the 1940's.

Welcome Home Committee festivities for Rossington men and women returning from W.W. 2. May 1946.

Alderman Hughes again, this time planting trees on Wadworth Lane. The boy with the shovel is John Drakeley. This is one of a set of photographs taken on this occasion.

Taken in about 1952, this photograph of the Labour Party Women's Section includes Mrs Royle, Mrs Waterhouse, Mrs Spence, Mrs Wright, Mrs Moran, Mrs Finnegan, Mrs Davies, Mrs Dobson, Mrs Jones, Mrs Windle, Mrs Wareing, Mrs McGuinness, Mrs B.

Rossington Colliery Canteen staff with the tables spread with Christmas fayre.

A presentation to Mr F. Mundy, for many years Sexton at St. Michael's Church, by Mr Hazel. Mr J. McGague is on the left.

An early photograph of the Wolf Cubs with, back row, C. Russon, R. Williams, D. Plaskett, ? Yates, ? Crook, A. Duffy. Middle row, J. Bennett, E. Pearson, J. Pine, F. Yates, G. Bird, J. Bird, C. Bell. Front row, R. Pownall, C. Wilson, P. Bell, R. Lewis.

Rossington 1st Scout Group. Another early photograph.

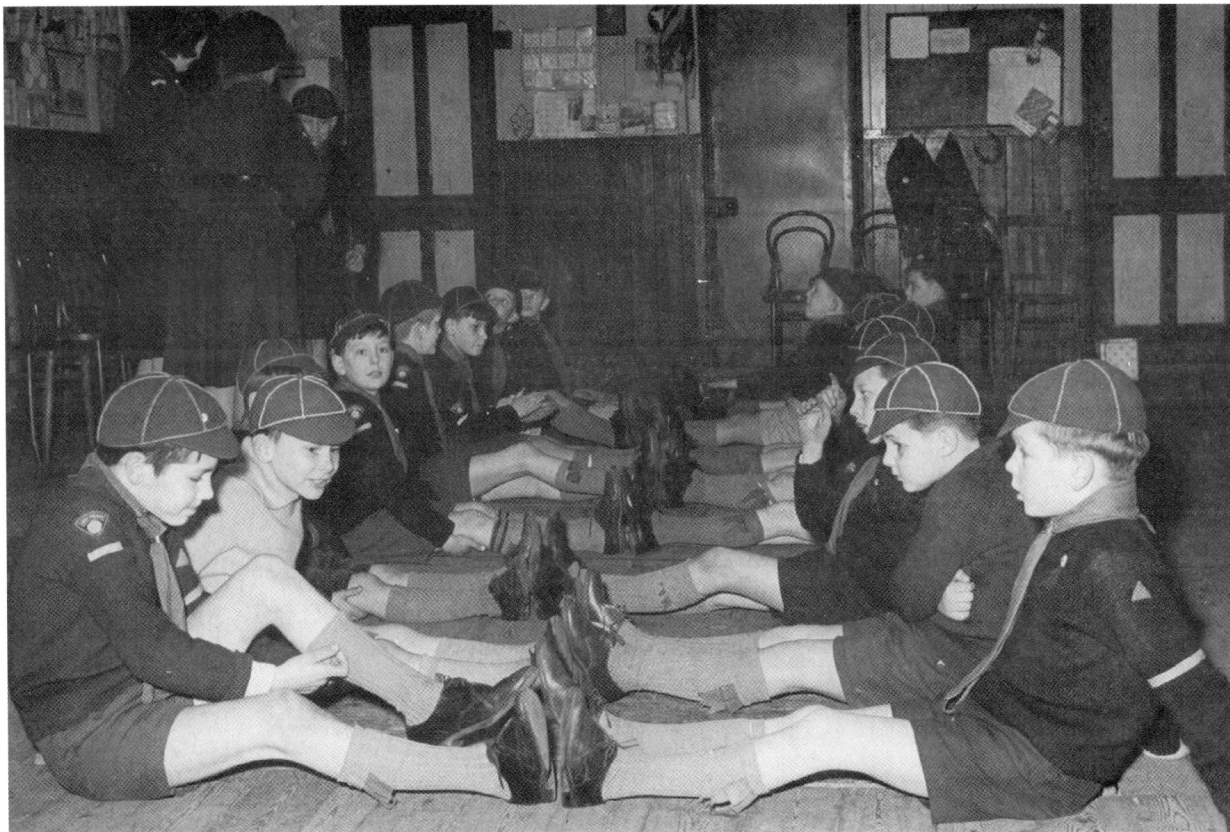

A 1950's group of Scouts perhaps in the Methodist Church room or St. Lukes' Church Hall. Pictured are Ian Boyd, David Malcolm. Donald Martin and Michael Ovington.

The Women's Branch of the British Legion on their Blackpool outing sometime after W.W. 2.

This group of British Legion ladies at Blackpool includes Mrs Moran, Mrs Hunter, Mrs Armstrong, Mrs Henderson, Mrs Askam and Mrs Fyall.

The Methodist Church Sunday School Anniversary 1946.

A Methodist Church outing. Names include Mrs Bramhald, Mrs Dinsley, Mrs Bradley, Mrs Cusworth, Mrs Lievesley, Mrs Coe, Mrs Attwell, Mrs Harkin and Mr and Mrs Fenton.

The Welfare Committee outing just after W.W. 2. Included are Ernest Jones, (Union Secretary), Mr Skinner, Bob Hughes, Norman Stanley, Mr Watkins (Under Manager), Jack Barton and Bill Trower (Clerk of the Welfare).

One of the many trips organised by Mrs Hetherington, this one to Skegness in about 1947. Included are Mrs Cox, Mrs Martin, Joyce Harvey, Mrs Harvey, Mrs Hetherington, Mrs Baker holding Maureen, Mrs Snaith, Mary Andrew, Alice Stockman with Janet, Mrs Telford and her baby. On the front row are Wilf and Jean Andrew, Jim and Frank Telford.

A cup winning team but all that is known about this one are two names - George Woodhouse (in the team strip, back row, right) and H. Webster on the front row, in the jersey.

Rossington was represented in the Hospital Cup Match Bowls Tournament against Armthorpe on 26th June, 1953. The team, on the back row, were, l. to r.- W. Littlewood, E. Smith, E. Quirk, J. Tickle, A. Robinson, J. Kay and J. Dyson. The Armthorpe team is on the front row.

Rossington's Joshua McGague talking to Don Valley M. P. Mr Tom Williams, at the Doncaster and District Labour Party Dinner, November, 1953.

The Youth Club soccer team 1953-4. Back row, l. to r. - D. Keomans, K. Mann, R. Makepeace,L.R. Cordon, E. Mugglestone, F. Bowes. Front, l. to r. - N. Wilkinson, J. Spencer, S. Matthews, B. Raw, J. Nelmes.

The Youth Club soccer team, 1956 - 7, back row, l. to r. - E. Pearson, E. Dixon, K. Mann, M. Makepeace, R. Cordon, E.

The Secondary Modern School Youth Club dance 1956.

This Colliery Officials' outing in the 1950's, includes Mr Quirk, J. Harkin, K. Jones and Mr Bradbury.

Mrs Wren, Mrs Baycock and Mrs Green, perhaps on an outing from the village, or are they at the Welfare?

An O.A.P. tea at the Welfare Hall, April 1961.

St. Luke's Youth Club group "The Nighthawkes", 1962. Keith Place, Kevin Pointon, Johnny Brown and Ian Ibberson.

Members of St. Michael's Church Choir in 1978 with Rector, Gordon Watt-Wyness, Mrs Mundie, Mrs J. Hilton and Mr Williams. Choristers include Anthony Halford, the Hilton girls, Shelagh Pain, the MacDonald girls and Rosemary Watt-Wyness.

Families and Friends

Jean and Wilf Andrew photographed with Veronica McGuinness (left) in about 1946 in the rear garden of 128, King George's Road. Note the 'concrete houses' in the background. These were demolished in the 1980's and the Skipwith Garden bungalows built on the site.

Emrys Andrew and his son Wilf in about 1946. Mr Andrew was a pit worker and suffered serious injuries in a roof fall in 1945.

Jean and Wilf Andrew outside their home 65, Allenby Crescent.

Connie, Ivy and Beryl Beardsley outside their home in Grantham Street. Mrs Connie Beardsley was 94 when she died in 1989 and will be remembered by many villagers.

Connie and Ivy Beardsley outside 18, Grantham Street in 1928. The girls worshipped at St. Luke's and were confirmed by the Bishop of Sheffield at St. Michael's.

Ivy Beardsley in the gardens of the Miners' Welfare in 1932. Ivy was a Sunday School Teacher in the village.

William Beardsley came in 1917 as a collier. The family lived in Streatfeild Crescent before moving to Grantham Street and left the village in the 1930's.

Mrs Charlotte Brown, wife of James Brown who purchased the Rossington Estate in 1838.

A St. Michael's wedding on 22nd July, 1944. Back, l. to r. - Ted Buddle, Mary Crosland, Norman Buddle, Mr Packham,, Mr Buddle, Vera Smith, Mrs Buddle, Mrs Packham. Front, l. to r. - Jean Andrew (Bridesmaid), Bill Packham (Groom), Peggy Buddle, Beryl Wilkes. The reception was held in the church hall. By coincidence, Mr and Mrs Packham were in the village to celebrate their Golden Wedding anniversary and supplied the date of their wedding for this caption.

J. D. Concannon photographed with his father William, at the family home at 6, Aberconway Crescent, in about 1938. John Dennis Concannon was born on 16th May, 1930. Educated at the Boys' School, he left the village in 1947 when he joined the Coldstream Guards, serving with them until 1953 in which year he married Ivy Wilson and became a member of the N.U.M. of which he was elected a Branch Official in 1960. Having settled in Mansfield he served on the Town Council from 1962 until 1966 when he was elected as the Labour M.P. for Mansfield. He held various positions during his political career - Assistant Government Whip 1968-70; Opposition Whip 1970-74; Vice Chamberlain to HM Household in 1974; Parliamentary Under Secretary of State for Northern Ireland 1974-76; Minister of State in the Northern Ireland Office 1976-79; Opposition Spokesman for Defence 1979-80 and for Northern Ireland 1980-85. He has been a member of the Commonwealth War Graves Commission since 1986.

Four generations of Concannons photographed in 1954.

Mr and Mrs Arthur Coulthread, Dorothy and Violet. Mr Coulthread was a well known cricketer who died in 1929. The family lived with Mrs Coulthread's grandmother in one of the cottages on Littleworth Lane, now *Coxley Mount.* Violet left St. Michael's School at the age of 14 to work at *Manor Farm* where she looked after Geoff Vaux, son of the Farmer.

Norman Fyall with his wife Mavis and daughter Alice, pictured outside their home on Allenby Crescent with W.W. 2 evacuee, Charlie Hines, from Leeds.

Mrs Eliza Ferris and her grandson David Phelps. Mrs Ferris's husband, William, was a sinker. This photograph was taken in 1948 just three weeks before her death. A member of the Chapel Bright Hour, Mrs Ferris held the distinction in the group of having knitted the most socks for W.W. 2 servicemen for which she received a certificate.

Doctor G. K. Graftdyke came to the village in 1935 from Leeds to succeed Dr Ritchie. He joined Dr Kane and became established as a true 'family doctor'. He was a talented pianist and organist who always took an interest in the village's musical activities. He retired in September 1975 and remained in the area until his death.

Mrs Hilda Graftdyke with Rosemary and Marie Smith outside the Graftdyke's home on West End Lane in about 1957. "Toots" was Mrs Graftdyke's pekinese.

William Ernest Jones was born in Derbyshire in 1895 and at the age of 14 started work at Southgate and Cresswell Collieries, Derbyshire. In 1910 he came to work at Rossington Colliery and in 1918 was appointed Branch Secretary of the Mineworkers' Union. Amongst his many activities and appointments, he was a Member of the Rural District and West Riding County Councils, a Magistrate, worked for the Ministry of Fuel and Power during W.W.2 and was President of the N.U.M. from 1954 until 1960. He was also a Member of the General Council of the T.U.C. for ten years from 1950, Secretary of the Miners' International Federation from 1959 to1969. He was awarded the O.B.E. in 1945 and the C.B.E. in 1961, the same year in which Leeds University conferred on him an Honorary Doctorate in Law. He married Annie Hall in 1918 and died in 1973.

A St. Michael's wedding group - Alf Green, Mary Green, Len and Elsie Green, Mrs Green in the 1940's.

Billy Lane came to the village from London with his father, a builder who helped construct the mining village. He is pictured somewhere in the village.

Martha McCourt married Edward Evans at St. Michael's Church on 25th July, 1937. Mr Evans had a sweet shop on West End Lane, at the top of Grantham Street. Pictured on the far right are Mr and Mrs E. Quirk. Dixon McCourt is standing behind the bride and Thomas McCourt is to the left of the groom. The kneeling bridesmaid is Audrey Quirk and to her right is Olive Quirk. What makes this photograph even more interesting is that it was taken in the Welfare Gardens on the site of the present swimming baths.

Ronald, Cyril, Joan and Mildred Marsh, McConnell Crescent, 1939. Father, Mr Peter Marsh was a colliery worker and the family lived first at 57, York Street. A photograph in "More Glimpses into the Past" shows Peter Marsh at the gate of number 57.

Harry Reaney delivering milk in Grange Lane.

Cousins Joyce Moss and Arthur Wood were members of St. Michael's Church Choir. c 1940. Arthur stayed with the family in the village during the war. Joyce remembers during the winter hymns at evensong were sung from lantern slides and sometimes the words were difficult to read in the blackout! She also remembers running home one Sunday afternoon during an air raid on Sheffield when the siren had sounded in the village. They ignored the Air Raid Warden's call to go into a shelter and ran all the way to Holmes Carr Road.

Ken Moss, Joyce's father. He was in the St. John's Ambulance Brigade for 42 years and Churchwarden at St. Luke's for some time. He became Safety Officer at the colliery when he retired from work.

Agent to the Rossington Estate, Mr. G. B. Shiffner, in his study at *Mount Pleasant.*

Mrs Georgina Mary Shiffner, daughter of Lt.-Col. William James Scarlett, whose brother was the Revd. James Williams Scarlett, Rector of St. Michael's from 1875 until 1910, married G. B. Shiffner in September 1893. She died in March 1949.

George Edward Shiffner and his younger brother, John. Known as Edward, the older brother was born in March 1901. He served in the Oxford and Buckinghamshire LightInfantry in W.W.2 and married Kathleen, daughter of Lt.-Col. Sir Edward Frederick, in March 1935. He died in July 1956. John Scarlett Shiffner was born in August 1910 and served as a Captain in the Royal Navy in W.W.2. He married Margaret Tullis in 1940 and died in 1981. The photograph was taken at the front door of *Mount Pleasant*.

John Shiffner mounted on "Yellow Peril" outside *Home Farm*.

Mary Bridger Shiffner with "Bump". Mary was born in 1898 and died in 1948. There were three other daughters:Marion Frances was born in April 1914 and died in 1947. Dorothy Mary (1894 - 1949) married George Godolphin Pelham, 2nd son of the 5th Earl of Chichester, in 1938. Eleanor Barbara Georgina established herself as an artist and died in 1981.

Mrs Taylor lived in one of the cottages which later became *Coxley Mount.* Her daughter married Arthur Coulthread.

Betty Vaux, youngest daughter of farmer Vaux of *Manor Farm.*

Margaret Vaux, older daughter of farmer Vaux, photographed at *Manor Farm.*

Geoff and Margaret Vaux with Miss Farr at *Manor Farm*.

William Winter-Dawson married Florence Hutton at St. Michael's Church. Here the group is pictured outside the Rosary Hall where the reception was held. Mavis Fyall is the bridesmaid on the right.

A group of local lads. Back, l. to r. - Arthur Clewes, Harry Bailey, "Smiler" Evans, Bill Frost. Front, l. to r.- Ray Dutton, Reg Whalley, Ken Dutton, Stan Dutton. The Duttons were a well known singing family.

Five men about town - William Concannon, standing, centre, pictured with four friends outside his grandparents' home on Firth Crescent.

In this group are, standing, Joe Milburn, Sid Cherry, Pat Grogan, Tommy Elliott, Reg Whalley, Johnny Grogan and Jimmy Dirkin. Seated are Mr Grogan Sn., Sheila Grogan and Mrs Grogan. Johnny Grogan won the "Miner's V.C." for saving a man's life in a pit disaster and died of his injuries aged 21.